Published by Creative Education and
Creative Paperbacks
P.O. Box 227, Mankato, Minnesota 56002
Creative Education and Creative Paperbacks
are imprints of The Creative Company
www.thecreativecompany.us

Design by The Design Lab
Production by Chelsey Luther
Art direction by Rita Marshall
Printed in the United States of America

Photographs by Alamy (Panther Media GmbH,
Rosanne Tackaberry), Dreamstime (Amilevin, Isselee,
Janossygergely, Kjersti Joergensen, Seaphotoart),
Getty Images (Tom Brakefield, Juan Carlos Vindas),
iStockphoto (Snic320), National Geographic Cre-
ative (GERRY ELLIS/ MINDEN PICTURES, STEPHEN
ST. JOHN), Shutterstock (Pavel Hlystov, Miceking)

Library of Congress Cataloging-in-Publication Data
Names: Bodden, Valerie.
Title: Sloths / Valerie Bodden.
Series: Amazing Animals.
Includes bibliographical references and index.
Summary: A basic exploration of the appearance,
behavior, and habitat of sloths, the slow-moving,
tree-dwelling mammals. Also included is a story from
folklore explaining why sloths do not build nests.
Identifiers: ISBN 978-1-60818-883-3 (hardcover)
/ ISBN 978-1-62832-499-0 (pbk) / ISBN 978-1-
56660-935-7 (eBook)

This title has been submitted for CIP processing under
LCCN 2017937606.

CCSS: RI.1.1, 2, 4, 5, 6, 7; RI.2.2, 5, 6, 7, 10;
RI.3.1, 5, 7, 8; RF.1.1, 3, 4; RF.2.3, 4

First Edition HC 9 8 7 6 5 4 3 2 1
First Edition PBK 9 8 7 6 5 4 3 2 1

SLOTHS

BY VALERIE BODDEN

CREATIVE EDUCATION • CREATIVE PAPERBACKS

Three-toed sloths have markings on their face, neck, or back

Sloths are the slowest **mammals** in the world. Two-toed sloths have two toes on their front feet. Three-toed sloths have three toes on their front feet.

mammals animals that have hair or fur and feed their babies with milk

Curved claws help sloths grip branches but make it hard to move on the ground

Sloths have small, rounded heads. They have brown or gray fur. **Algae** (*AL-jee*) grows in their fur. A sloth's front legs are longer than its back legs. Sloths' feet have sharp claws.

algae plantlike organisms that have no leaves, roots, or stems and grow in damp or wet places

Most three-toed sloths are about 18 to 23 inches (45.7–58.4 cm) long. They weigh about 8 pounds (3.6 kg). Two-toed sloths are usually bigger. Some weigh almost 20 pounds (9.1 kg).

Three-toed sloths weigh about half a pound (0.2 kg) at birth

All sloths live in Central and South America. They make their homes high in rainforest trees. They look for places where the trees grow close together.

Sloths learn to crawl hand-over-hand from their mothers

Sloths eat mostly leaves.
Sometimes they eat flowers and fruit, too. They get most of the water they need from the plants they eat.

Cecropia leaves make up most of three-toed sloths' diets

A mother sloth hangs upside down when she has a baby. The baby climbs onto the mother's stomach. She carries the baby through the trees. After about a year, the baby sloth leaves its mother. Sloths can live 15 to 20 years.

A sloth baby begins eating solid foods around 10 days old

Sloths spend their days alone in the trees. They slide along branches to find new leaves. They rest a lot, too. Sloths sleep up to 20 hours a day.

Sloths curl up in a ball when they sleep to hide from birds of prey

Sloths have poor hearing and vision but an excellent sense of smell

The ground is not a safe place for sloths. **Predators** like jaguars prowl there. Sloths climb down from their tree only once a week. They go to the bathroom. Then they climb back up.

predators animals that kill and eat other animals

A sloth can hold itself in a tree using just one set of claws

Not many people get to see sloths in real life. Sloths are hard to spot in the wild. Only a few zoos keep sloths. This is because sloths can get sick in **captivity**. It is fun to learn about these slow-moving creatures!

captivity being kept in a pen or cage, rather than being left to roam free in the wild

A Sloth Story

Why don't sloths build nests? People from Brazil told a story about this. Long ago, there was a bad storm. The sloth fathers said they would build nests the next day. But the next day was sunny. The fathers forgot to build nests. The same thing happened when it stormed again. So the forgetful sloths never built nests.

Read More

Borgert-Spaniol, Megan. *Sloths*. Minneapolis: Bellwether Media, 2016.

Schuetz, Kari. *Baby Sloths*. Minneapolis: Bellwether Media, 2014.

Websites

Enchanted Learning: All About Sloths
http://www.enchantedlearning.com/subjects/mammals/sloth/
This site has sloth facts and a picture to color.

San Diego Zoo Kids: Two-Toed Sloth
http://kids.sandiegozoo.org/animals/mammals/two-toed-sloth
Learn more about two-toed sloths.

Note: Every effort has been made to ensure that the websites listed above are suitable for children, that they have educational value, and that they contain no inappropriate material. However, because of the nature of the Internet, it is impossible to guarantee that these sites will remain active indefinitely or that their contents will not be altered.